Wild Britain

Hedgerows

Louise and Richard Spilsbury

www.heinemann.co.uk
Visit our website to find out more information about Heinemann Library books.

To order:
 Phone 44 (0) 1865 888066
 Send a fax to 44 (0) 1865 314091
 Visit the Heinemann Bookshop at www.heinemann.co.uk to browse our catalogue and order online.

First published in Great Britain by Heinemann Library,
Halley Court, Jordan Hill, Oxford OX2 8EJ
a division of Reed Educational and Professional Publishing Ltd.
Heinemann is a registered trademark of Reed Educational & Professional Publishing Ltd.

OXFORD MELBOURNE AUCKLAND JOHANNESBURG BLANTYRE
GABORONE IBADAN PORTSMOUTH (NH) USA CHICAGO

Designed by Celia Floyd
Illustrations by Alan Fraser
Originated by Dot Gradations
Printed in Hong Kong/China

ISBN 0 431 03902 X (hardback)   ISBN 0 431 03909 7 (paperback)
06 05 04 03 02 01   06 05 04 03 02 01
10 9 8 7 6 5 4 3 2   10 9 8 7 6 5 4 3 2 1

British Library Cataloguing in Publication Data
Spilsbury, Louise
    Hedgerows. – (Wild Britain)
    1. Windbreaks, shelter belts, etc. – Great Britain – Juvenile literature
    2. Hedgerow ecology – Great Britain – Juvenile literature
    3. Hedges – Great Britain – Juvenile literature
    I. Title II. Spilsbury, Richard
    577.5'55'0941

Acknowledgements

To our own young wildlife enthusiasts, Miles and Harriet.

The Publishers would like to thank the following for permission to reproduce photographs:
Bruce Coleman: Kim Taylor pp5, 11, P Clement p10, Andrew Purcell pp12, 17, Gordon Langsbury p19, p29; FLPA: Roger Wilmshurst p16, E & D Hosking p27; Garden & Wildlife Matters: p4; NHPA: Laurie Campbell p9, 25, Mike Lane p21, Manfred Danegger p26; Oxford Scientific Films: David Cayless p6, Terry Middleton p7, Dennis Green p8, David Wrigglesworth p13, Niall Benvie p14, Ian West p15, John Cooke p18, D J Saunders p20, Arthur Butler p22, Michael Leach p23, William Paton p24, p28

Cover photograph reproduced with permission of Harry Smith Collection

Our thanks to Andrew Solway for his comments in the preparation of this book.

Every effort has been made to contact copyright holders of any material reproduced in this book. Any omissions will be rectified in subsequent printings if notice is given to the Publisher.

Contents

Any words appearing in the text in bold, **like this**, are explained in the Glossary.

What is a hedgerow?

Some hedgerows separate fields from town buildings.

hedgerow

Hedgerows are high, narrow strips of land covered in trees and other plants. They mark the edge of a field, road or garden. They are used instead of walls or fences.

A habitat provides living things, like this thrush and its young, with food, water and **shelter**.

A **habitat** is the natural home of a group of plants and animals. In this book we look at some of the plants and animals that live, grow and **reproduce** in hedgerow habitats.

5

Types of hedgerow

This hedge is a row of trees that was once part of a wood.

Some hedgerows are very old. They are often strips of woodland left when the main wood was cleared for farming. Rows of trees were left to divide the fields.

Hedgerows separate fields or land from roads or paths.

Newer hedgerows are often made from one kind of tree such as hazel, or a shrub like privet. Hedgerows may also be made of banks of earth with plants growing on them.

Changes

In spring this hedgerow is full of flowers like foxgloves and honeysuckle.

In spring and summer the sunshine helps flowering plants to grow. **Insects** come to feed on the leaves and **nectar**. Animals come to feed on the insects and the plants.

We can eat some autumn fruits, like blackberries, but not others. This fieldfare is eating berries.

In autumn leaves change colour and fall off many trees. This is also the **season** for **fruits** and berries. Many birds come to the hedgerows to eat the different fruits.

Living there

Small birds and **mammals**, like this mouse, eat nuts and berries from the hedgerow plants.

The bottom of the hedgerow provides **shelter** and food for many living things. The plants above block the light, keeping the bottom of the hedgerow damp and dark.

Butterflies, moths and other **insects** come to drink **nectar** from hedgerow flowers.

Higher up, there is more light. Birds make nests in the branches of the trees. They eat the nuts, **seeds** and **fruits** which grow on the trees and other plants.

Hedgerow plants

Nuts are the **seeds** of the hazel tree. Seeds that fall may grow into new hazel plants.

Many different plants grow in hedgerows. Some, like the hazel tree, form the main part of the hedgerow and give it its shape. Hedgerow animals eat the nuts of the hazel tree when they fall in autumn.

Inside blackberry **fruits** are seeds that may grow into new bramble plants.

All plants need light to grow. Climbing plants, like honeysuckle and brambles, have weak **stems**. They need the support of other hedgerow plants to grow tall to reach the light.

Wild flowers

These primroses and other wild flowers grow in the damp shady parts of a hedgerow.

Some wild flowers, like primroses, grow in a hedgerow because it provides **shelter** from the wind. Wild flowers grow from **roots** in the soil, near the bottom of the hedgerow.

The foxgloves in this hedgerow have dark pink petals that form trumpet-shaped flowers.

The **stem** of a flowering plant acts like a drinking straw. It takes water and **nutrients** from the roots to the rest of the plant. The petals that form the flowers are often brightly coloured.

Moths and caterpillars

To **reproduce**, the cinnabar moth lays its eggs on leaves.

The cinnabar moth feeds on the **nectar** of hedgerow flowers. The moth's bright red and black colours warn birds that they taste nasty, so birds leave them alone.

The cinnabar moth caterpillar also tastes nasty to birds.

The caterpillars that **hatch** from cinnabar moth eggs have orange and black stripes. They eat leaves and grow quickly. Then they wrap themselves in a **chrysalis**, where they stay until they turn into a moth.

Beetles and spiders

This burying beetle is feeding on a dead animal it has found at the bottom of a hedgerow.

Beetles have hard wing cases that cover most of the body. Some eat plants, both living and dead. Others eat dead animals and other **insects**.

The wasp's feet are stuck and tangled in the web so it cannot escape the spider.

Many spiders live in hedgerows because there are lots of flies and other insects for them to feed on. Spiders build webs to trap their food.

Wrens and blackbirds

The hedgerow provides cover for birds, like this wren, as they search for food.

The wren is small enough to flutter through the bottom layers of the hedgerow. It eats berries and **seeds**, and small **insects**, spiders and worms from among the fallen leaves.

The male blackbird catches worms with his sharp beak.

Larger birds can eat bigger living things.
Blackbirds eat snails and grasshoppers too,
as well as blackberries in autumn.

Dunnocks and cuckoos

Birds' eggs are different colours. Dunnock eggs are sky blue.

Hedgerows provide **shelter** and protection for the nests of many birds. Dunnocks build their grass nests low down in hedges. This hides them from larger birds that try to eat their eggs.

This dunnock is feeding the cuckoo. She thinks it is her chick.

Cuckoos do not build their own nests at all. The female lays her eggs in the nests of other birds. When cuckoo chicks **hatch** out, they push the other eggs out of the nest. The mother bird feeds them instead.

Hedgehogs

Hedgehogs move from place to place under the cover of the bottom layers of the hedgerow.

The hedgehog has a pointed snout to sniff out its food. Hedgehogs come out at night to eat slugs and small animals among the fallen leaves.

Hedgehogs roll into a prickly ball if attacked by another animal. This is how they protect themselves.

A hedgehog's back is covered with special thick hairs called spines. These sharp spines protect them from other animals. Sadly, many hedgehogs are killed by cars as they scurry along roadside hedges.

Weasels and shrews

The weasel can run and bound quickly along the lower edges of the hedgerow.

The weasel's long, slim body helps it crawl down small holes in hedgerows to chase mice, rats and voles. The weasel has a good sense of smell to sniff out its food.

This is a shrew looking after its young in its nest.

Weasels do not usually eat shrews, because they taste horrible to them. Shrews eat **insects** and small animals from the bottom of the hedgerow using their sharp teeth.

Dangers

When hedgerows are cut down, plants and animals lose their homes and food supply.

Many hedgerows have been cut down to make bigger fields for modern farm machines. Others are cut down because hedges are not needed on farms that no longer keep animals.

Pollution and litter can harm the plants and animals that live in hedgerows like this one.

All hedgerows need to be trimmed. But if they are cut back in spring, plants may be lost because they have not had time to make **seeds**. Also birds' nests may be destroyed.

Food chains

All plants and animals in a hedgerow **habitat** are linked through the food they eat. Food chains show how different living things are linked. Here is one example.

The wren eats the spider.

The spider eats the wasp.

The artwork on this page is not to scale.

Glossary

chrysalis   stage in growth before insect becomes an adult (also called pupa)

fruit   the part of a plant that holds its seeds

habitat   the natural home of a group of plants and animals

hatch   to be born from an egg

insects   six-legged minibeasts with bodies divided into three sections: head, thorax (chest) and abdomen (stomach)

mammals   group of animals that includes humans. All mammals feed their babies with their own milk and have some fur or hair on their bodies.

nectar   sweet sugary juice in the centre of a flower

nutrients   food that gives living things the goodness they need to live and grow

pollution   something that poisons or damages air, water or land

reproduce   when plants and animals make young just like themselves

roots   parts of a plant that grow underground. They take in water and goodness from the soil.

season   there are four seasons in a year: spring, summer, autumn and winter

seeds   these are made by a plant and released to grow into new plants

shelter   somewhere safe to stay, live and have young

stem   the stalk that holds up the leaves, flowers and fruit of a plant

Index